Bus Driver Discipline On The Road As You're Rolling

Bus Driver Discipline On The Road As You're Rolling

Collin J. Allen

iUniverse, Inc.
New York Lincoln Shanghai

Bus Driver Discipline On The Road As You're Rolling

iUniverse books may be ordered through booksellers or by contacting:

iUniverse
2021 Pine Lake Road, Suite 100
Lincoln, NE 68512
www.iuniverse.com
1-800-Authors (1-800-288-4677)

ISBN-13: 978-0-595-39246-9 (pbk)
ISBN-13: 978-0-595-83638-3 (ebk)
ISBN-10: 0-595-39246-6 (pbk)
ISBN-10: 0-595-83638-0 (ebk)

Printed in the United States of America

Contents

Introduction

To the parents and other bus drivers who took the time to provide me with this much needed information. This book has been designed to give a bus driver tips and other resources in order to work with the children on a more professional level. Some drivers put themselves down by saying, "I am just a bus driver". You are not "just a bus driver," you are a very special person who can do many tasks and still successfully do what you do. Many times you become the teacher, counselor, doctor, and or parent of many of the children you transport everyday. So never look at yourself as just a bus driver anymore. Look at yourself as a well-rounded special person who loves their job and has so much to offer each and everyone of those kids you come in contact with.

I have been a bus driver for twelve years now, and during that time it has been a learning experience for me. When I substituted for a year and a half, the kids were not a problem for me. The problem was the bus. I was having to leave one job where I cared a great deal about people. Then I was having to enter another job where I had to control this big yellow bus. Finally I could truly enjoy the kids. As I helped to better the health of sick people, it became the most inspiring part of my life; However, when My own health problems arose I had to move on and it seam like I lost a part of myself. I was having to retrain my mind to deal with only kids. Then I could reach for more knowledge in order to better serve and relate to students who have behavior problems, learning disabilites, or low self-esteem. Children are so pure and innocent. Their inner beauty becomes real, expecially the ones with problem. After taking on a full-time route I began to monitor the different behaviors and how I could better interact with my students.

Parents have personally thanked me for doing what I felt worked best when their children were on my bus. This attitude of working from my heart has served me well. Reaching out to others has helped me to understand that each child has different needs and that each child needs must be met. Every driver has his or her way of managing discipline on their bus. While the bus is in motion, you have fifty to sixty students sitting behind you and no monitor to assist you, therefore you as the driver must be mentally prepared. You must be prepared for every student on that bus to forget about the rules, and the consequences they face. The peer pressure on the students are very high these days. Please note carefully that there is always a ringleader on each bus and this contributes to behavioral problems. When they can get the other kids to turn on then you as the driver needs to gain control. You have to know right away what to do, especially when you are the only one in control of the bus. The matterials I have gathered for this book will hopefully help each of you to become more aware of bus driver discipline on the road as your're rolling.

Chapter One

Each student on your bus will behave differently. How you classify them can determine the outcome. No behavior is a forgotten behavior but you can make a change in what the outcome will be and at the same time earn respect from the students. Write-up after write-up is not the answer for every situation. For example, for every student that yells out the bus window or throws paper wads at another student a write-up may or may not be the solution. Sometimes I may find that talking to a child helps change their behavior as oppose to yelling at them. Perhaps using a soft, but stern voice gets their attention. Many times when a student is acting out in an inappropriate way, ninety-nine percent of the time it is due to peer pressure or lack of attention in the home. This leads me to believe if you get to the root of the problem then you see that there is a reason behind that childs behavior and possibly this may or maynot resolve that individuals problems on your bus.

Every once in a while you will have a student with a disruptive type of behavior that is completely out of control. In a situation like this you must make sure you monitor that student closely, and always remain incontrol for disclplinary actions, always keep an information log and report all behavior problems to the school principal. Even take time to consult with the school guidance counselor, so that he or she can be aware of childs behavior. Remember the more information you know about the student the better you can assist the student. You can keep order on your bus and help a student who is reaching out. You are the driver and there may be no assistance available for you but there is hope for the child and it begins with you. The following are three steps to seat placement and child invlovement on your bus in order to "keep order". The first step is to never place the student in the back of the bus, because you can never slove the problem if the student remain there. The second step is to never place the student in the seat right behind you, because the student will get on your nerves. This also keeps the child out of your space. The third step is to always place the student on your passenger side, second seat by the window not close to your aisle side, so you know where the child is sitting at all times. Finally, try to find that special student who can be a leader for the troubled student and ask them to sit with the student every day. There will be a high energy level with this troubled child, but keep in mind that this student is not your normal child when this is happening. They love to get involved in issues that can draw some attention to them. If you can keep your problem child out of the lime light, then all of your other problems can be under control. If this student has problems getting along with several other students on the bus then rearrange your seating to keep order. You will need to log who sits where, for your own records. You may have to place names above seat, so that the students can keep tract of their seat as well. This does take time but it will be worth it if you love order on your bus.

Peer pressure is extremely high in elementary, middle and high school now. Make sure you are aware of the behaviors of your students on your bus and address them on a daily basis. No student is better than another. Nor is one smarter, because they all have special traits to offer. If you share ideas such as those then it will give the students something to think about before they speak out to are about. Name-calling and backtalking are two of the most common situations dealt with on the bus. You will find that the student looking for attention will say mean things to hurt no one but themselves. They may call themselves names or talk about other students to make themseleves appear bigger and badder than they really are. Then they may try to get other students to say bad things about others. Some kids join in just so they don't feel left out. Some are very talkative and can become the life of your bus. You should make sure you are aware of what is taking place at all times and address those issues; Everyday you will log what took place on each run in your little black or green book. It is also helpful to read back to all students on the next day what took place on your bus and what you expect out of them today. Send home warning sheets that you have made up. You may want to list the things that happens on the bus so that you don't forget for future reference or to refer back to. Ask the students to talk with their parent or guardian and bring a signed note back to you. If they mention their parent or guardian doesn't care about what they do, an alternative would be to tell them to bring a signed note from their principal. It is always best to give the school information about how you deal with behavior on your bus so that you and the school can be on the same wavelength when dealing with a childs behavior on a bus. This clears up any confusion that may arise. Body language speaks loud and is a tool that gives away when students are lying, misbehaving, hurt, sick, or just lost in their own little world. When a child is locked in emotions, they may ask questions or talk to you because you make them feel safe. Be there for them and try not to let your emotions keep you from seeing the whole picture. One time I had a student on my bus who cried every day because they didn't want to go to school or they didn't get a chance to wear what they wanted to. At first I thought something was happening at home to make this child act this way. I came to find out it was all about what he wanted to do. Then I had another student looking out the window who was dying of cancer and whose head was shaved bald, she wore wigs but didn't like them. At one point in my life I was having health problems and my head had to be Shaved, so I started wearing hats. Therefore, I understood her pain and knew exactly where she was coming from. I really sympathized with her and this made my student feel good about herself and she spent her last days being that special little girl whom I knew and loved.

Your behavior says a lot about how your students behave on your bus. If you are a distant person then your students will never address you with respect because they already have the impression that you don't care and you are just driving for a paycheck. The way to get around the disrespect is to get more involved with your students on the bus. Start by saying "good morning" with a smile on your face as they load the bus and "good bye" as they are leaving the bus. Feel free to get up out of your seat and greet your students as they are exiting the bus. You should try to learn each student's name and address them as they enter your bus and exit, because I find that this makes them feel special. Even if you just learn the first name, watch the smile on their face or their eyes light up. Some things that you can say to get a smile are, for exmple have a good day," or "if I don't see you this evening have a great weekend". "have a safe" and " happy holiday"; and " see all of you in the year 2005". It's ok to let some of your own emotion show, because it shows that you are human just like the students you service. Remember you're not a robot and you are their bus driver. These kids have feelings, too, and they will show you once in a while by hugging you. Your problem child may even tell you that he or she loves you. Keep in mind that it means thank you for making time for them when everyone else stops caring. Just look in your mirror with a smile to let them know that you hear what's being said. Treat all of your students the same by showing the same amount of care toward everyone. Never treat one differently from the other even if your own child is riding your bus. My own child has ridden my bus and at one time I had to write him up. Misbehaving will not be tolerated on my bus. I believe the principal thought I had lost my mind when they saw that misconduct note come across their desk. I honestly felt I did the right thing; whats fair was fair and I let my students know that I will treat all my students the same, even when it comes to my own son.

Keep updating yourself on new information each year and stay informed on what is happening in and out of schools this way you wont be left out of the loop and can better interact with your students. Your own behavior can make a child dislike or love you. If you are following all the rules and information that is available to you, along with following your heart then you won't go wrong. There will be times that you are at your lowest and feel you just cannot take any more disruption or behavior problems. You may even find yourself telling a student they will be written up and not have a good reason for writing them up. When you get to that point, check yourself out because you were not focused on what has taken place. Remmeber you should not give up on a student or give into the situation. All you know is that you just did not feel well when the kids acted up on that day. I find myself telling the students the next day that for example, John Doe misbehaved badly and I didn't fell my best so I told John Doe that he had a write up. I also told John Doe that I'm going to give him one more chance today to prove to me that chance today to show you know the rules on the bus, and if I see that he refuses to obey the rules today there will be an immediately write up. Then there's that high energy time when I'm so playful and my students feed off my energy level. This can be fun, but there's always that one who takes things a little too far. When you call that student out, they act like they've lost their best friend. You have to keep in mind who is the adult. That's when I tell my student you will either hate me or love me, because I have to stay in charge of my bus. I love you, but there can only be one captain on this bus.

I talk to them a lot about being a team player and what they can do to help me get them home and to school safely. Not all of my students want to be a team players so I have team leaders. Ninety percent of the time you will have more team players than you have leaders. If you can control the atmosphere or attitude on your bus then your students will be more than happy and willing to be a team players.

No day is ever the same. Where do you go when you have a student out of control? What steps do you take in order to get the child some help? Make sure you go through the chain of command first. Start with the principal of that school, guidance counselor, and director of transportation. Most of all you will have to gain some patience because it may take a while before your problem is resolved. Make sure that you have documentation on the child's behavior explaining when the problem started and what you did to assist the child. When that problem occurred. Never go into an office without written documentation for the supervisor, The following documentation backs up what you said happened. Have all of your facts written down, because you will forget from day to day. I remember one time I put off writing in my little black book about what occurred with one of my students and the next day the child asked me what was going to be his punishment. I did not have enough clear facts in my head, so I could not give him an answer. Never let a student know you forgot what they did. I told him to sit up front and asked him if he talked to his parent about his behavior on the bus. I knew the whole time I didn't remember what the child did. When he took his last step off the bus he turned around and said I am sorry for what came out of my mouth yesterday. I immediately knew he had said a bad word. Never tell a child it is okay when it is not right to say or do something when they are out of parent sight. You will find out that even your own kids are not angels when they are not in your presence.

"ADDED POEMS FOR BUS DRIVERS WHO CARE"

The Special Bus Driver

Drivers keeps their eyes and ears open so they can do their best.

Their heart is better than a machine, it's the real thing.

Bus drivers lets their kids share their feelings when no one else will Listen.

Bus drivers are Moms and Dads, when your baby cries the driver handles it all.

Wipes their eyes and tells a story the same time.

Bus drivers are special drivers and that's all there is to it.

Special, special drivers come with their hearts broken and put back together with plenty of hugs.

Collin

Allen

1/14/1993

School Bus Drivers

Bus Drivers are loving and caring people, they don't push and shove, they are proud to say," they are Bus Drivers".

The smiles and tears that the kids bring to us are all worthwhile.

When the hugs and kisses are given when you turn your head say's something special.

Bus Drivers are not a clock or some kind of ticking machine.

They look, listen and feel the heat when it is time to take control.

Bus Drivers are good-hearted people with big hearts. They care about the little things as well as the big things.

A Thought For Everyone

"You may not be a Bus Driver, but the progress that we see in a child can result only from the fact that someone showed enough concern to care about them."

Collin

Allen

KESPA

Member

2/4/1998

At middle school age there are so many changes in the middle school child. Sometimes parents just don't notice their child's behavior until it is too late. As a bus driver you need to be informal at all times and most of the time the child will tell you the problem. The child might say: "I can do what I want", "who cares", or "you don't tell me what to do". The one you hear the most is "I don't care what you do, my parent will eat you alive".

This is the age I feel that kids need guidance and help the most, because they are more impressionable. They start playing the role of an adult, but yet they're still growing and learning. It is so hard for them to distinguish what's right and wrong. Especially, when they are trying to fit in with their peers. When they are in sixth grade they are so playful and loud. Then they're in the seventh grade and wish they did know which way to go. They are trying to fit in with the eight graders and will do anything to get attention. Most of the time, they end up get in trouble. The eight grader get very demanding and feel they can do no wrong. They tend to talk back and refuse to follow the rules. Always address each matter with the student. If you have a child who wants to be the center of attention, give it to them, but do it in a way that everyone on your bus can be involved. Even have your students vote on what was said and turn the matter into a civil debate. Then the attention they wanted is no longer what they wanted. You will then see that the student will give you more respect and have better respect for himself. I am so proactive in what goes on my bus, I came up with my own discipline sheet in 1995 for the route I have been on for twelve years. It had to be something I could use for elementary, middle and high school.

I would circle what the child did and if this was their first warning or what.

Date: _____

Dear Parent or Guardian:

I want to share a concern about _____conduct on my bus. Your child has misbehaved on the bus. They have been asked to write a statement about the misconduct, and also tell how he or she can be more responsible in the future.

Student statement:

_____

_____

_____

_____

_____Behavior problem

1. Not following directions the first time they were given
2. Throwing paper
3. Not staying in their seat and feet on the floor while the bus is in motion.
4. Pushing, shoving other students
5. Writing on bus seat or damage to the bus
6. Swearing, using rude gestures, teasing other students
7. Not sitting in assigned seat
8. Playing around on the bus

9. Too Loud

10. Screaming on the bus

Please talk to your child about their behavior and have them return this note to me promptly. Thank you very much in helping me get your child safely to school and back home to you.

Sincerely

Mrs. Allen

Parent Signature_____

Contact Number

Incident: 1ST 2ND 3RD

Date:_____

Dear Parent/Guardian:

You child's behavior caused a problem today. They refused to follow the rules . This is a warning before reporting the incident to school. Please talk to you child about their behavior and have them return their warning sheet back the next day. If this warning sheet is not returned the next day, they will have to be turned in to the school Principal.

Your child has been ask to tell you the truth about what took place on the bus today.

Student statement:

_____

_____

_____

_____

_____

_____

_____

_____

_____

_____

_____

_____

_____

_____

_____

_____

_____

_____

_____

Student name: _____

Grade: _____

Warning: 1st 2nd 3rd

Parent Signature: _____

Contact Number
000-0000
Driver: Mrs. Allen

August 2006

Date: _____

Dear Parent/Guardian:
Your child had a behavioral problem today. He (She) refused to follow the bus rules. This is a warning before reporting the incident to school. Please talk to your child about this matter and have them return their warning sheet back the next day. If the warning sheet is not returned the next day, your child will have to be turned in to the school Principal.

Student name: _____

Grade: _____School:_____

Not staying in their seat
Hitting

Too loud
Talking back
Not follow the rules
Playing around on the bus
Would not obey the Bus Driver

Parent Signature: _____

Contact Number
000-0000

Warning: 1st 2nd 3rd

Chapter Two

STEPS TO TAKE TO GET IN CONTROL OF YOUR BUS

Never let a student feel they have the upper hand. If this happens it means they are fully in control of your bus. When they come to you talking at the highest level of their voice, give them their space. At the same time they should receive just enough space to be embraced by their peer group. For example; a student mouthing off to you every-day. You give him a miscounduct note when he does it, but take a look at another option that may work in this situation. Ask your bus load of students what should be done about the situation right in front of him. This will make the student think about what he or she is doing next, then the child if they heard what the other students suggested? Tell the misbehaving student what you think should be done about his behavior problem. After you have given the child three choices, then repeat them to him. His peer group might feel he should no longer ride the bus with this type of behavior. You feel something needs to be done about the situation, and perhaps you can make an example out of him to the others. Here is my response to the student: "you are a very bright person with a few behavior problems. We as the group will try to work out, before extreme measure have to be taken. You will have an assigned seat for a few day as we monitor your behavior. If you fail to work with us then I will have to do my job and turn you into the school principal. Last, I question him. Do you understand what we as a team are trying to do for you?"

You can also give out your three warning sheets, then fill out a bus misconduct report. Show the student their conduct sheet and make sure you have recorded dates of everything they did on the bus up to this point. Let the student know, if you don't see any changes in them, that you will be turning them into the principal. Ninety-nine percent of the time they will change their behavior but there will be one percent that will try you. When that happens, stand by your words or you will have every child on your bus trying you.

Remember to give out your warning sheets. Then make sure that your students are turning the sheets back in to you. You can tell who your problem child will be when you give the first note and they do not return it the next day or they make up an excuse about where it is. Make notes of who you given warning sheet to. When they are returned, file them away, so if you ever have to meet with a parent or you have a question about the student's behavior, you will have your notes to fall back on.

You should keep a record book like the teachers have in the classrooms. You place every student's name in it that rides your bus and keep a daily attendance of each child using your two back seats as a reward. In your record book place an "B-" for Back seat check for a good day and "X-" for a bad day, "-" not here today and "T-" treats today.

The last resort is groups. My students hate it when I put them in groups.

This is were I elect a group leader for the week and add 12 students to each group. Each group is given 10 points for the month. Every time a student breaks the bus rules, then points are taken away. The group at the end of the week will receive some type of reward for their group. It may be one day YMCA passes, a pan pizza certificate, or coke. I have discovered that when I do the group activity I get more feedback from my students on what is taking place on my bus. Sometimes I get a little too much feedback. The game becomes so intense that my student are talking about it on other buses and down the hallways at school. This makes me feel good about what I am trying to accomplish because the students who are talking are the ones who are creating the problem on my bus . Normally, three months before school is out, I play the group game. This games has helped kept many of my students from being suspended from riding the bus. They have to face their group when they misbehave, instead of the driver having to get on the student in which they eventually end up in the principal's office. When I can get the student to see their mistake and what they can do to control it, I've done something worthwhile instead of just sitting in that seat and driving. Going the extra mile takes hard work and sometimes I feel like creativity is what is needed for this job. Then I come up with more ideas for my students who I care about.

STAYING FOCUSED ON YOUR BUS

There have been many days that has been hard for me to concentrate on driving that big yellow bus. During some of the most stressful times my life seemed like it was falling apart as I made each stop to pick up a child or to drop one off. It seemed like my days were weeks going on and on. I am a Spirit-driven person and try to live a Christian filled lifestyle with my focus on God. My prayen life is very instrumental in my role as a bus driver. I pray before I get on the bus and I thanked God when I get off the bus in the evening. When you have so many little bodies sitting behind you and their voices are blending together and one or two of them are failing to follow the bus rules, your mind is lost in another world. At stressful times such as this a driver must remember to stay foucsed on your bus in this world. So my choice is Jesus Christ, the Lord. I have discovered that God has given me the grace and peace in everything I do and I have done.

When a student sees you have lost your focus they tend to get out of control and it spirals form there. Before you know it you have stepped over the line. This is why you have to check yourself each day and every time you step onto your bus. The questions I ask myself everyday are "Am I ready to do my job today? Can I do the job today? How would I rate my driving on a scale of 1 to 10?" There are times I am not a ten or a five but I make myself aware of that and use extra effort to become a ten. If you are not too proud to admit to yourself what has taken place in your life, then you have what it takes to be that driver with a ten. This is where you have to talk to yourself in order to know what level you are on before driving the bus off the lot.

You can not control the different cycles your life will go through, nor can you dictate how your life will be. The Bible gives good guidelines for a successful life. It gives us the wisdom to grow and leads us toward peace and joy. All of our blessings will follow us in what we do. This is how I keep my focus everyday as I live life to the fullest and try to direct the child who needs my help. The Lord knows I am not a perfect angel, but I don't have a heart that has hate in it either. I want to live the best life that God has prepared for me. At the same time I want to bring security, love, and happiness to a child's life. I see students as a gift from God and a blessing to the world that we know nothing of. When I reflect onto my life, I feel I am living the best life that I can. I want a child to see that life can be as pleasant as you make it.

MIDDLE SCHOOL, LOVE THEM OR LEAVE YOUR JOB

There have been times that I question myself about the job I do. It hurts me when I get questions about how I do my job, or when parents accuse me of not liking or picking on their child. I love all my kids and would do anything to protect them. So when a parent comes to me in such a foolish way, it hurts my feelings and I am at a lost for words. I have learned in the past few years that some parents will believe their child even when they know the child is in the wrong and it sounds crazy to them, too. They fail to follow their hearts. This is when they let their child get the upper hand. I have learned to stand my ground when the parent loses their focus. I have the child come back on my bus the next day. The child is proud of what their parent said and they really want to rule my bus. It is hard to stay focused when I've lost the support of the parent. I never let that child move too far away from me because I know they will try anything on my bus. I do tell the child they have created a problem and I'm sorry, but I can not trust them at this point. So now before I can allow the child to move to another seat I have to be able to trust them. With my middle school students it is very important that you like them. When you don't trust them, they feel that you don't like them. This is where I have to be able to talk to them a little at a time. As they question my decisions I make sure we are on the same page about what is required from them.

DON'T IGNORE THE CHILD BEHAVIOR

At middle school age there will be many changes in the student's life.

It's up to the parent and the driver to take notice of the child's behavior right away. If you fail to notice what is going with your students, then this is when you have failed as a driver. You will have an out-of-control bus load of students. They want to play the role of an adult, but they're still growing and learning. It gets hard sometimes for them to distinguish what is right and wrong. Here a few changes that will be seen with the sixth, seventh and eighth graders.

- Very playful

- Get very demanding

- Talk back

- Refuse to follow the bus rules

- Certain changes in their clothing and hair styles or image

If you find you have a student showing any of these traits, it's best to address the matter before it gets out of hand. Try not to wait too long because the longer you wait the bigger the problem will become. Always keep in mind you are the driver and the rules have to be followed.

HIGH SCHOOL STUDENTS NEED LEADERSHIP BY MAKING THEM MORE RESPONSIBLE ON YOUR BUS

Many of my high school students play the role of a big brother or big sister. They take care of the small kids on my bus and calm the middle school students by communicating on the level that each student will understand. I let them play an important role in being proactive on the bus. During the eleven years that I have driven the same route, I told my students that we are a family and we have to communicate with each other; and at the same time build trust within our bus.

There's not a day that goes by that I don't have something nice to say about someone on my bus. This could be when I see my high school students taking a leading role in assisting a younger child. I may have a student getting on the bus crying because their parents would not let them bring something to school. One of my high school students might ask the younger child to sit with them. They begin to talk with them about what took place before getting on the bus and they let me know the younger child is okay. The little things they do to helps me to focus on the next task at hand and drive my bus and not worry.

WHAT TO DO WHEN A STUDENT HAS THE UPPER HAND

The good new is to know that you are not perfect. You may have to slow your thinking process down and cut back on the coffee. It's okay to start back at the beginning and take it one step at a time. Make sure that you are consistent and fair with your students. Find a listening ear from somewhere, because you will need it. None of your kids are bad, take that word out of your vocabulary. They are just kids who sometimes need tough love. When students get out of sight of their parent, they become little misdirected because they fail to tell their parent the truth. This is when most of problem arise. Be consistent and don't change the rules just to fit one child, whose parent may blame you for their child's problem. They may be the best student in the classroom at school and become the worst problem on the bus. Keep in mind that if you look closely at each one of your students, there will be a change in them each year. I have seen the quiet children turn into the strangest people in a year's time and one of my loudest disrespectful students turn into one of the most respectful on the bus.

Chapter Three

A PRAYER A DAY KEEPS ME IN CONTROL EACH DAY

Before I start my day I read each morning from a devotional book and search my Bible to reinforce what I had read. My life had been spared three times or more. The last one was when the tornado hit Owensboro, Kentucky in 2002. I was one of whom was trapped by the tornado. The tornado wind stopped my bus in his track. It stopped me from moving as I was trying my hardest to get to a safer place. It literally moved my bus to one side. I was frightened and stayed in my seat as it trapped me in. The windshield wiper snapped off the back window and middle window popped out. The whole time I remained in that seat calling "Jesus" name. The louder the tornado got, the louder I called "Jesus" name. I remember the bus was getting ready to flip over on one side and I said," Oh no, Jesus, Jesus, as tears rolled down my face. I know how prayer works. Each time God has given me one more blessing and I have to share myself with the most priceless gift of all, his children. I love what I do, but in the meantime, prayer keeps me alive in order to stay focused in his world.

SHOWING EACH STUDENT YOU CARE

Many kids do go unnoticed with behavior that is out-of-control on your bus. The question to ask is: what can you do? How do you deal with this child everyday? There are good parents and bad parenting and this adds to some of our students problems. I hope these tips can help you to control your bus on the days you feel that only you can do your job. Follow some of these tips and see if it changes your bus.

Remember to pray that you can control your kids and let them see that you care. Star by saying, "good morning" and "good-bye" in the evening. Even if hey never say a word know that they are listening. If you are a new driver, good luck and if you are an old driver, have faith in your job. Change the old ways and start a new beginning.

978-0-595-39246-9
0-595-39246-6